INTRODUCTION

The Sneaker Coloring Book is a collection of line drawings of the most famous sneaker models from 1916 to the present day. They can be used, as the name suggests, to color in, to redesign, and to customize. The collection is an overview of 100 shoe silhouettes that have been particularly successful, shaped the market, or distinguished themselves through their innovation. Basic information such as manufacturer, model name, category, and date of the first launch is listed for each model.

The market for sneakers has grown enormously over the last few decades. For some time now, versions of old classics have been relaunched in various color and material combinations. This diversity is important for companies wishing to cover all kinds of market segments defined by criteria such as the age, culture, and musical or sporting interests of the target group.

The shoe industry uses silhouette drawings—so called line arts—to communicate internally the many design variations with corresponding departments and for ordering at the manufacturing sites. The specifications of the respective collection are recorded on these silhouette drawings. Inspired by such technical documents, we have illustrated and collated a unique collection of accurate line arts of 100 models in chronological order.

The term 'sneaker' refers to sports shoes, or shoe models inspired by sports, that are worn in a fashion context. The way for sneaker history was paved in the 1840s by Charles Goodyear and his invention of vulcanization. This was first used by the manufacturer British Rubber Co. Ltd. (later Dunlop) to bind linen with rubber, resulting in 'Sand Shoes' for the beach. The term was coined by marketing expert Henry Nelson McKinney in 1917 because of the rubber sole—all other outdoor shoes, with the exception of moccasins, had a louder tread.

The collecting of sneakers and the sneaker 'cult' were long unknown phenomena and the passion of a few sneaker enthusiasts only. But as sneakers became identified with sports stars, as with the Converse All Star launched in 1917, and endorsed by basketball player Chuck Taylor from 1923, they rapidly became more popular. To this day, the Converse All Star is still available in its original design and is claimed to be the most successful sneaker ever created. Everyday life without sneakers became unimaginable; they

became an important and established fashion item, with many people owning several pairs for different occasions. Followers of certain subcultures began to identify with certain models, and their individual requirements led to the demand of a large and varied range of sneakers being designed.

At the same time, other companies like New Balance from Massachusetts (orthopaedic trainers), or the Dassler brothers, were also producing sneakers but in more limited numbers. After the Second World War, Onitsuka Tiger (Kihachiro Onitsuka), Adidas (Adolf Dassler), and Puma (Rudolf Dassler) were founded. From then on the market became international and small shoe workshops grew into large enterprises due to increased demand. These companies were constantly looking for innovations to fulfil the various requirements of different sports. Through advertising, well-placed sponsorship, and

fashion trends, sneakers slowly started to capture the imagination of the street. By the end of the 1960s, they had become socially acceptable and a part of everyday life. They were made popular by youth cultures who used them as a sign of rebellion, as a fashion statement, or to distinguish themselves from the establishment.

Nike was founded in the 1970s and became world market leader by the 1980s. Until then, the industry had offered many variations of the black/white sneaker design but companies now started to include new colors and materials in their ranges. The most influential subcultures—the hip-hop movement, the so-called 'casuals,' and the skateboard scene—chose sneakers as their trademark. They gave sport shoes a face, helping them to become the successful status symbol, and fashion item they are today.

THE SNEAKER COLOURING BOOK

ILLUSTRATIONS & TEXT BY
D. JAROSCH & H. KLINGEL

WWW.PKNTS.COM/TSCB

Published in 2010 by Laurence King Publishing Ltd
361–373 City Road
London EC1V 1LR
United Kingdom
Tel: + 44 20 7841 6900
Fax: + 44 20 7841 6910
e-mail: enquiries@laurenceking.com
www.laurenceking.com

A catalog record for this book is available from the British Library.

ISBN: 978-1-85669-667-8

Design: Daniel Jarosch and Henrik Klingel, PKNTS

Printed in China

Front cover: Line drawings of Adidas Gazelle 2, Puma Clyde, Nike Air Epic, Nike Air Force I Hi, Adidas Decade Hi, Onitsuka Tiger Mexico 66, Converse All Star and Reebok Freestyle Hi

There are various options in categorizing shoes. The silhouette gives determining clues about the origin of the sneakers, or rather the sport for which they have been developed. Listed here are the three biggest categories.

The silhouette of running shoes is relatively flat. The rubber sole is often glued directly on to the upper in the toe area. The cushioning consists of an EVA wedge, and for the upper, mainly light and breathable materials are used.

Basketball shoes are usually Hi-Cuts made from leather. Due to the high athleticism and great strain in this sport, most basketball shoes are robust and compact. Special types of rubber have been developed for the soles to avoid marking the court floor and to enhance cushioning.

Traditionally, almost all tennis shoes are white. The rubber sole has a very fine herringbone profile for games on clay courts and a smooth profile for indoor courts. Most tennis shoes are Low-Cuts.

INSTRUCTIONS

The following pages form the core of the book—the coloring pages of 100 sneakers by 18 different manufacturers. The position of the tabbed numbers on the right margin refer to the period of their launch (see key at back of book). All of the templates can be used to color in and customize straight away. There are no limits to your creativity; whether you want to use markers, crayons, ink, or watercolors and brushes. Once colored in, the artist can date and sign their work in the columns 'Colorist' and 'Date.' All 100 coloring pages can easily be torn out along the perforation in order to hang the finished artwork. This also makes it very easy to scan or copy the templates.

And for those who like the book as it is, well, you now have a collection of the 100 best-known sneakers in black and white line drawings, so drop those pens and just enjoy *The Sneaker Coloring Book*.

KEDS

MODEL	CHAMPION
LAUNCH	1916
CATEGORY	TENNIS

COLORIST	
DATE	

CONVERSE

MODEL	ALL STAR
LAUNCH	1917
CATEGORY	BASKETBALL

COLORIST	
DATE	

002

ADIDAS	
MODEL	SAMBA
LAUNCH	1950
CATEGORY	SOCCER
COLORIST	
DATE	

PRO-KEDS	
MODEL	COURT KING
LAUNCH	1955
CATEGORY	BASKETBALL
COLORIST	
DATE	

DUNLOP	
MODEL	VOLLEY INT.
LAUNCH	1959
CATEGORY	VOLLEYBALL
COLORIST	
DATE	

ONITSUKA TIGER

MODEL	NIPPON 60
LAUNCH	1960
CATEGORY	TRAINING

COLORIST	
DATE	

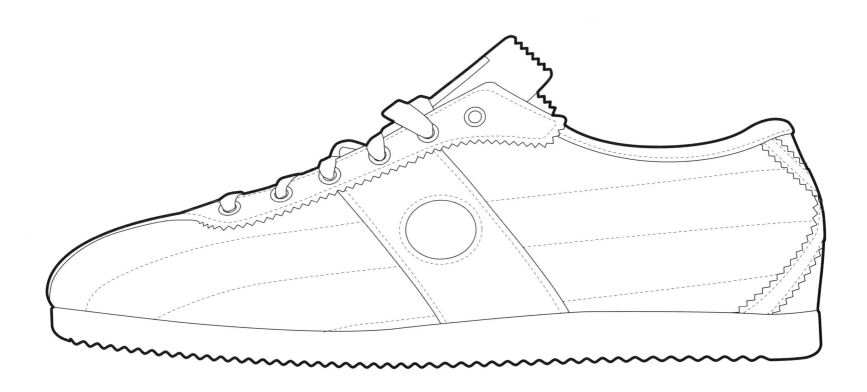

LACOSTE	
MODEL	RENÉ LACOSTE
LAUNCH	1963
CATEGORY	TENNIS
COLORIST	
DATE	

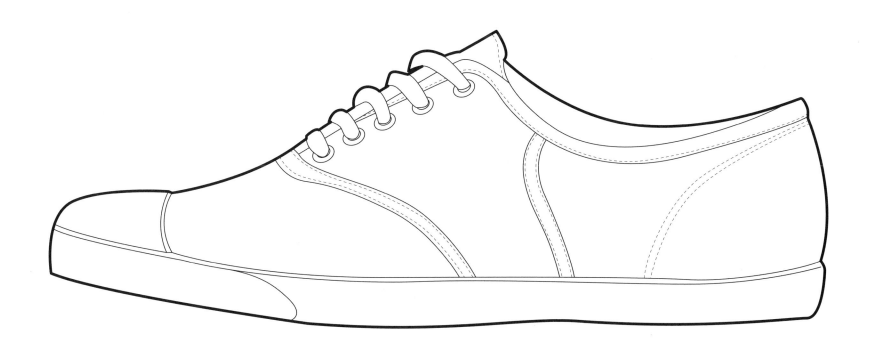

ADIDAS	
MODEL	STAN SMITH
LAUNCH	1964
CATEGORY	TENNIS
COLORIST	
DATE	

ADIDAS	
MODEL	ROM
LAUNCH	1965
CATEGORY	RUNNING
COLORIST	
DATE	

KAWASAKI	
MODEL	PLAYERS 23
LAUNCH	1965
CATEGORY	INDOOR
COLORIST	
DATE	

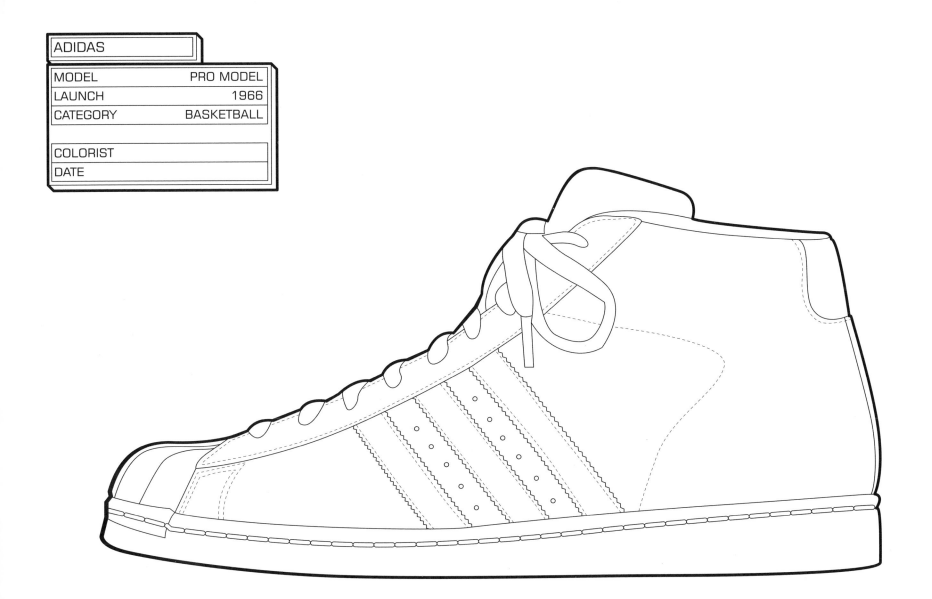

ADIDAS

MODEL	PRO MODEL
LAUNCH	1966
CATEGORY	BASKETBALL
COLORIST	
DATE	

011

012

ONITSUKA TIGER	

MODEL	MEXICO 66
LAUNCH	1966
CATEGORY	RUNNING
COLORIST	
DATE	

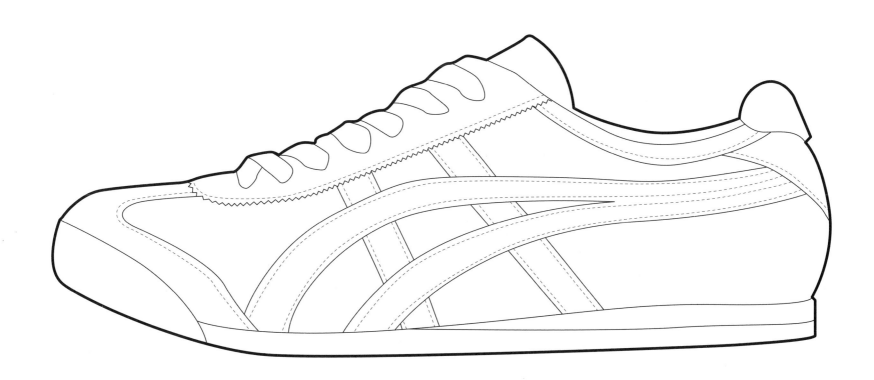

TRETORN	
MODEL	NYLITE
LAUNCH	1967
CATEGORY	TENNIS
COLORIST	
DATE	

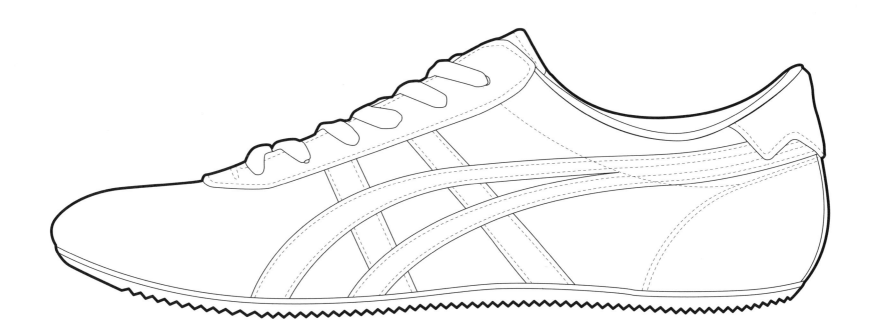

ONITSUKA TIGER

MODEL	TAI-CHI
LAUNCH	1968
CATEGORY	MARTIAL ARTS

COLORIST	
DATE	

015

PUMA	
MODEL	CLYDE
LAUNCH	1968
CATEGORY	BASKETBALL
COLORIST	
DATE	

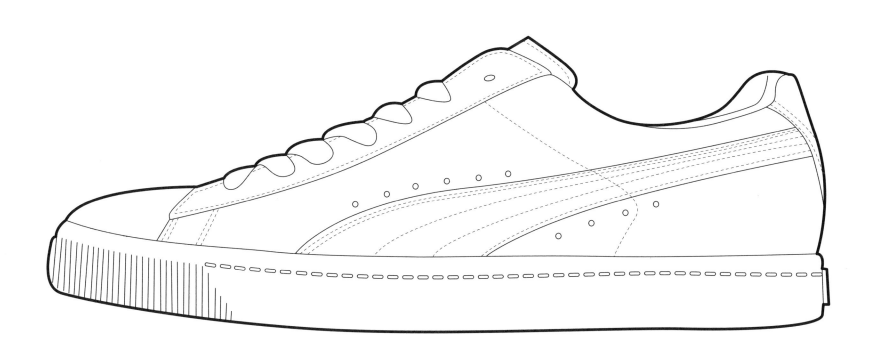

ADIDAS

MODEL	ROD LAVER
LAUNCH	1970
CATEGORY	TENNIS

COLORIST	
DATE	

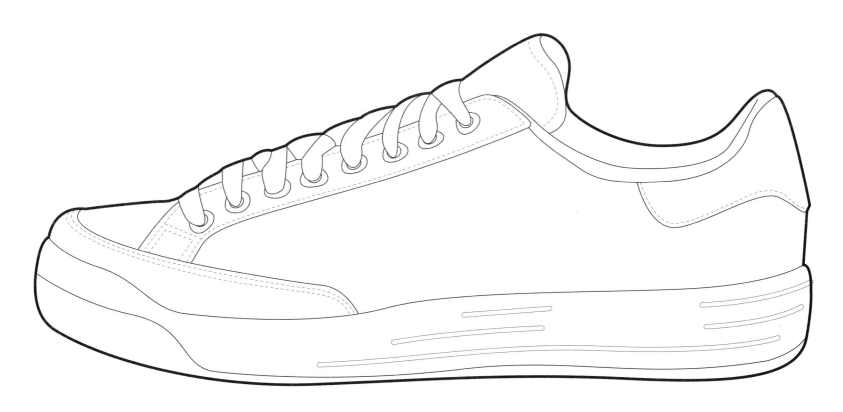

ADIDAS

MODEL	JABBAR HI
LAUNCH	1971
CATEGORY	BASKETBALL
COLORIST	
DATE	

ADIDAS	
MODEL	NIZZA HI
LAUNCH	1972
CATEGORY	BASKETBALL
COLORIST	
DATE	

NIKE	

MODEL	BLAZER
LAUNCH	1972
CATEGORY	BASKETBALL
COLORIST	
DATE	

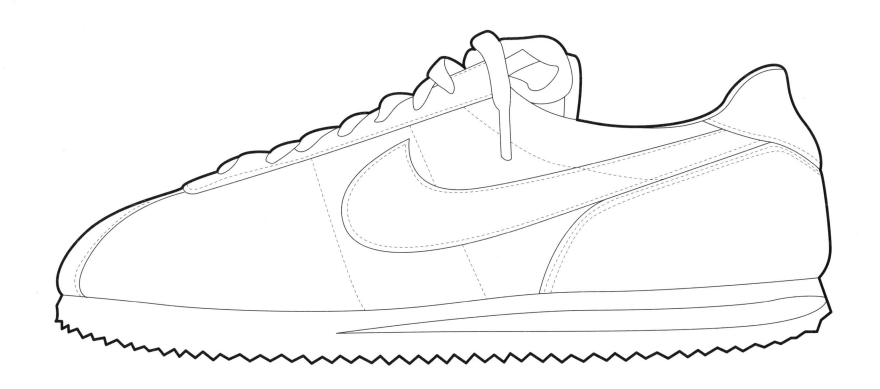

PUMA	
MODEL	MUNICH
LAUNCH	1972
CATEGORY	RUNNING
COLORIST	
DATE	

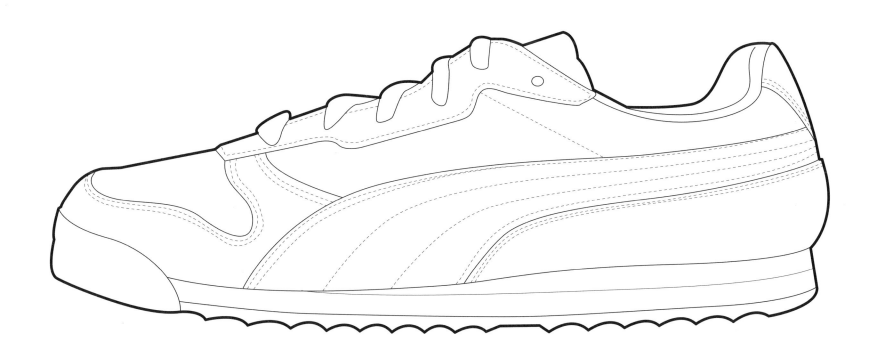

PUMA	

MODEL	RS 100
LAUNCH	1972
CATEGORY	RUNNING
COLORIST	
DATE	

MODEL	WAFFLE TRAINER
LAUNCH	1973
CATEGORY	RUNNING

COLORIST	
DATE	

VANS		
MODEL		SLIP-ON
LAUNCH		1973
CATEGORY		SKATEBOARDING
COLORIST		
DATE		

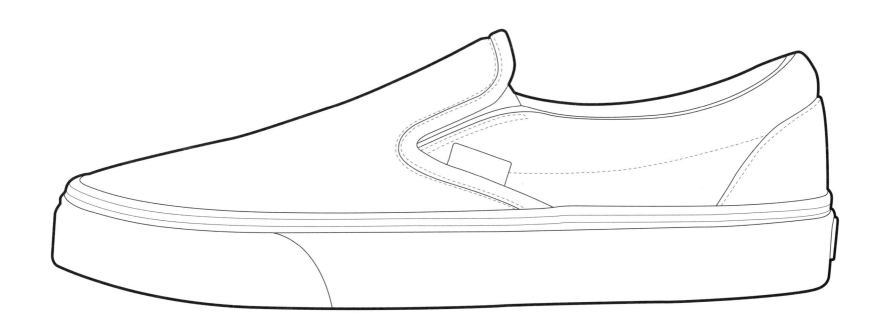

CONVERSE	
MODEL	ONE STAR
LAUNCH	1974
CATEGORY	BASKETBALL
COLORIST	
DATE	

MODEL	TRAINER
LAUNCH	1974
CATEGORY	BASKETBALL
COLORIST	
DATE	

MODEL	FABRE BL-L
LAUNCH	1974
CATEGORY	BASKETBALL

COLORIST	
DATE	

MODEL	RUNSPARK
LAUNCH	1974
CATEGORY	RUNNING
COLORIST	
DATE	

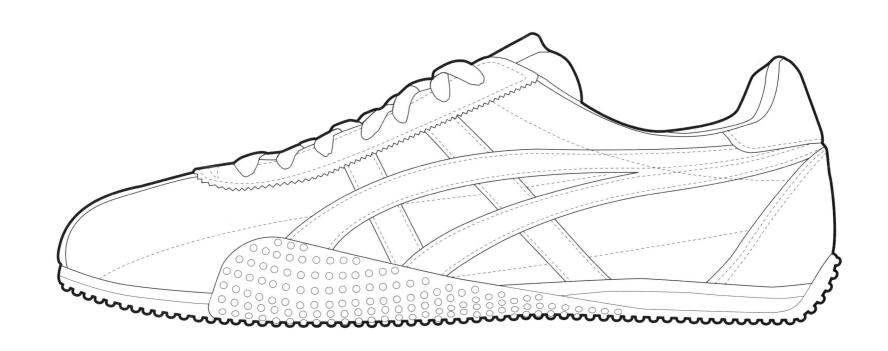

PONY

MODEL	TOP STAR
LAUNCH	1975
CATEGORY	BASKETBALL

COLORIST	
DATE	

NEW BALANCE	
MODEL	M320
LAUNCH	1976
CATEGORY	RUNNING
COLORIST	
DATE	

VANS

MODEL	ERA
LAUNCH	1976
CATEGORY	SKATEBOARDING
COLORIST	
DATE	

NIKE	
MODEL	OREGON
LAUNCH	1977
CATEGORY	RUNNING
COLORIST	
DATE	

ADIDAS	
MODEL	ADRIA
LAUNCH	1978
CATEGORY	TENNIS
COLORIST	
DATE	

ADIDAS	
MODEL	INDOOR TENNIS
LAUNCH	1978
CATEGORY	INDOOR
COLORIST	
DATE	

PUMA	

MODEL	ARGENTINA
LAUNCH	1978
CATEGORY	SOCCER
COLORIST	
DATE	

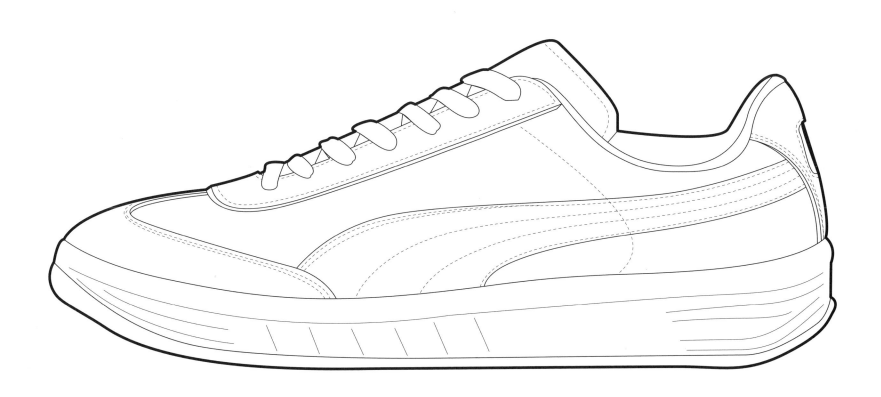

VANS

MODEL	SK8 HI
LAUNCH	1978
CATEGORY	SKATEBOARDING

COLORIST	
DATE	

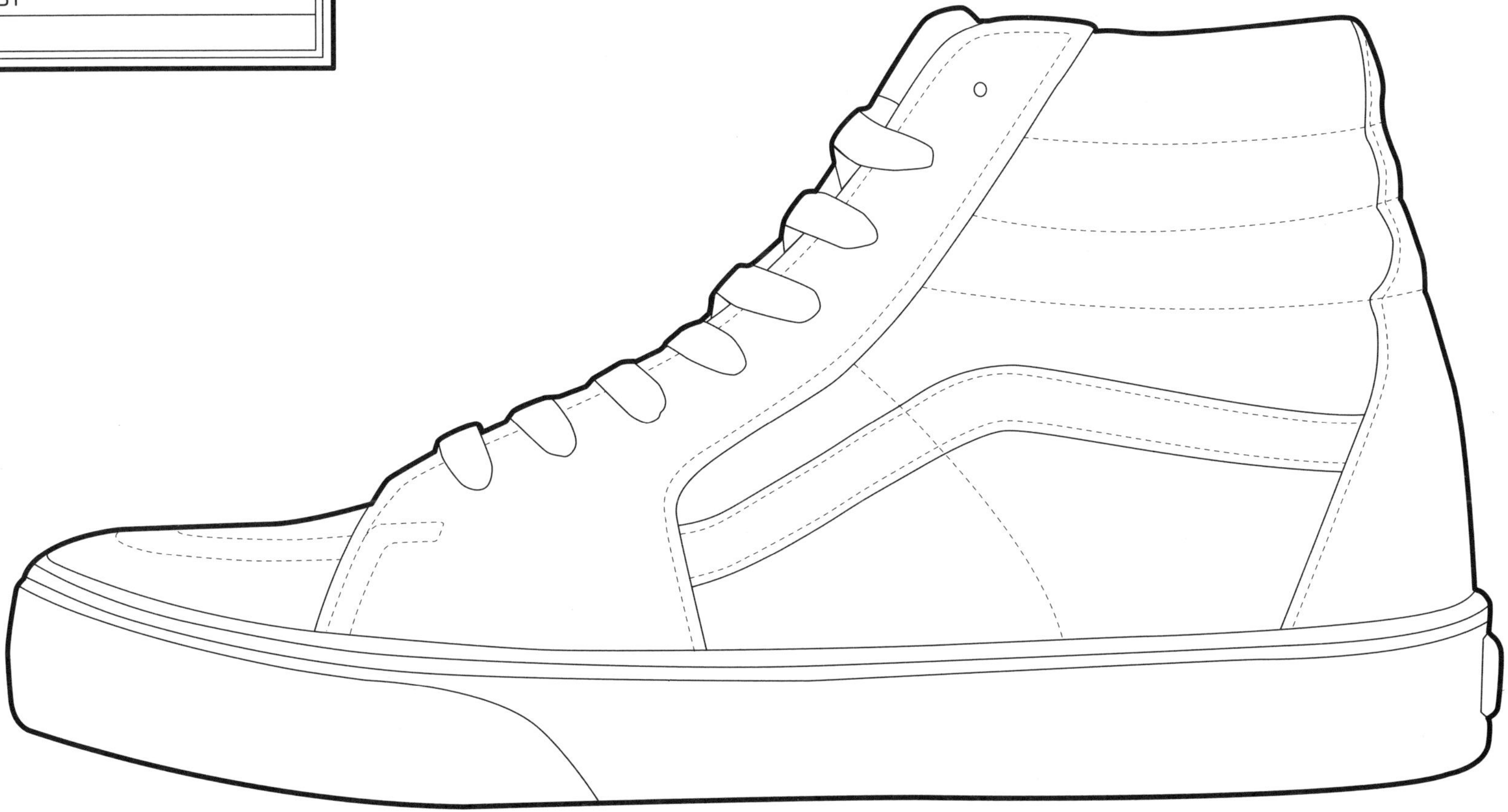

ADIDAS

MODEL	TOP TEN
LAUNCH	1979
CATEGORY	BASKETBALL
COLORIST	
DATE	

CONVERSE

MODEL	ALL STAR PRO
LAUNCH	1979
CATEGORY	BASKETBALL

COLORIST	
DATE	

PRO-KEDS	
MODEL	SHOTMAKER
LAUNCH	1979
CATEGORY	BASKETBALL
COLORIST	
DATE	

ADIDAS

MODEL	GAZELLE 2
LAUNCH	1980
CATEGORY	TRAINING

COLORIST	
DATE	

ADIDAS

MODEL	MARATHON
LAUNCH	1980
CATEGORY	RUNNING

COLORIST	
DATE	

043

ADIDAS	

MODEL	HONEY MID
LAUNCH	1981
CATEGORY	BASKETBALL

COLORIST	
DATE	

NIKE

MODEL	DYNASTY
LAUNCH	1981
CATEGORY	BASKETBALL

COLORIST	
DATE	

MODEL	TOUCH
LAUNCH	1981
CATEGORY	RUNNING

COLORIST	
DATE	

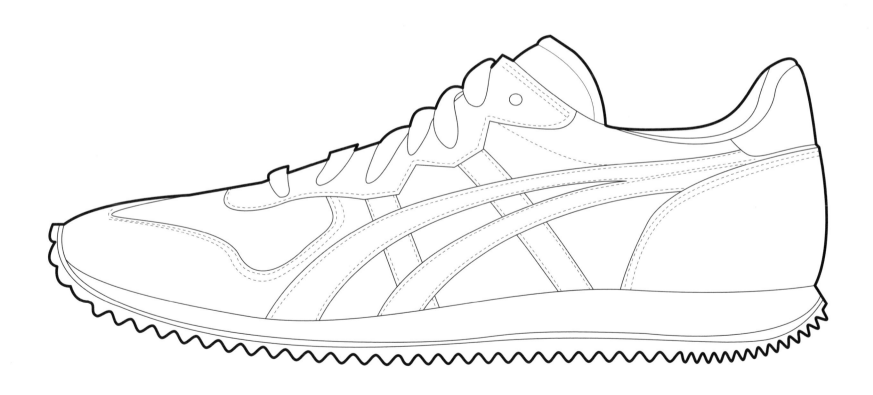

ONITSUKA TIGER

MODEL	ULTIMATE 81
LAUNCH	1981
CATEGORY	RUNNING
COLORIST	
DATE	

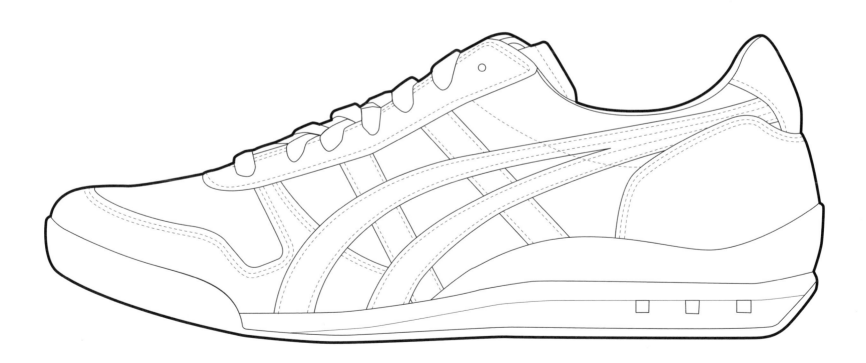

PUMA	
MODEL	CABANA RACER
LAUNCH	1981
CATEGORY	RUNNING
COLORIST	
DATE	

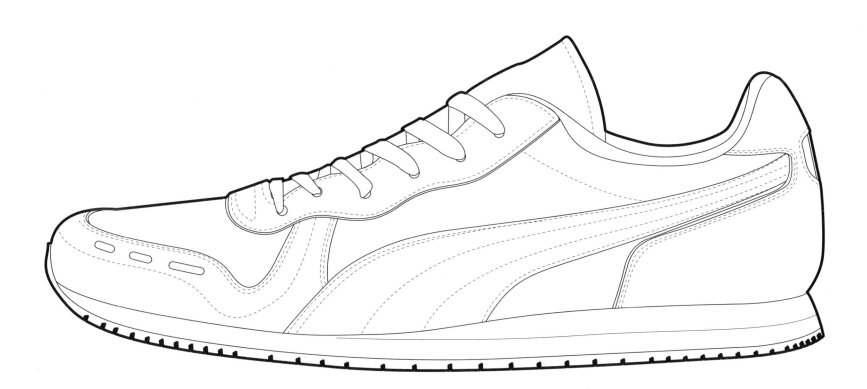

MODEL	M410
LAUNCH	1982
CATEGORY	RUNNING

COLORIST	
DATE	

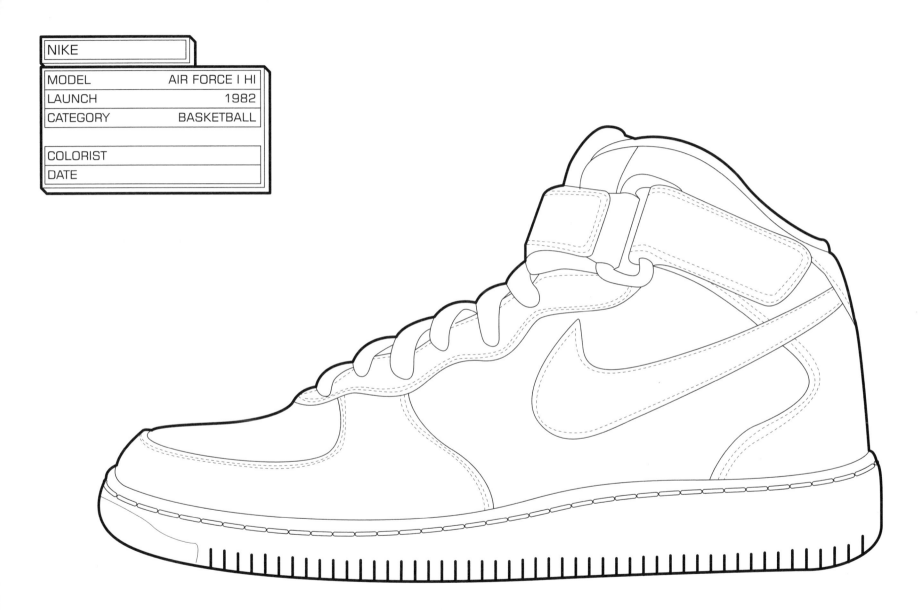

NIKE	
MODEL	AIR FORCE I HI
LAUNCH	1982
CATEGORY	BASKETBALL
COLORIST	
DATE	

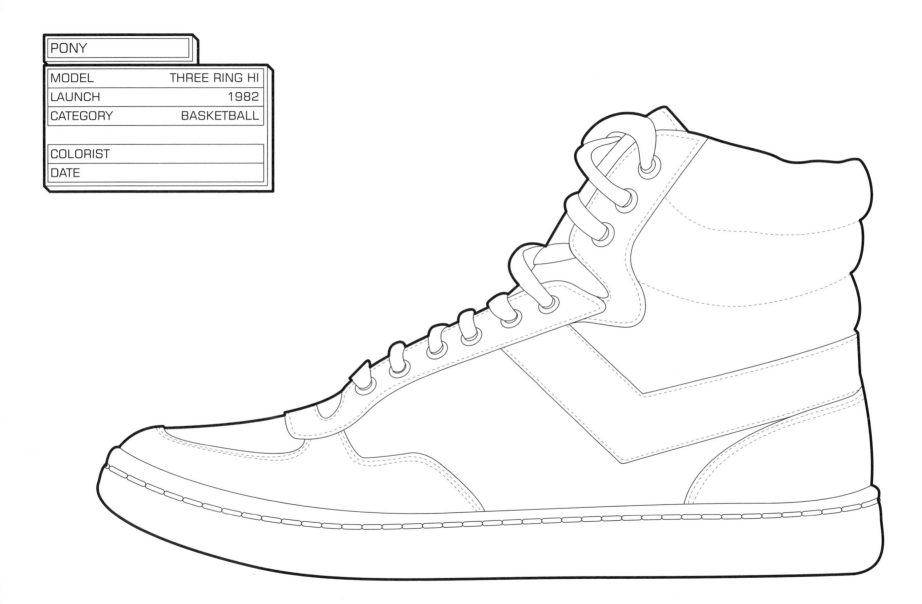

PONY

MODEL	THREE RING HI
LAUNCH	1982
CATEGORY	BASKETBALL

COLORIST	
DATE	

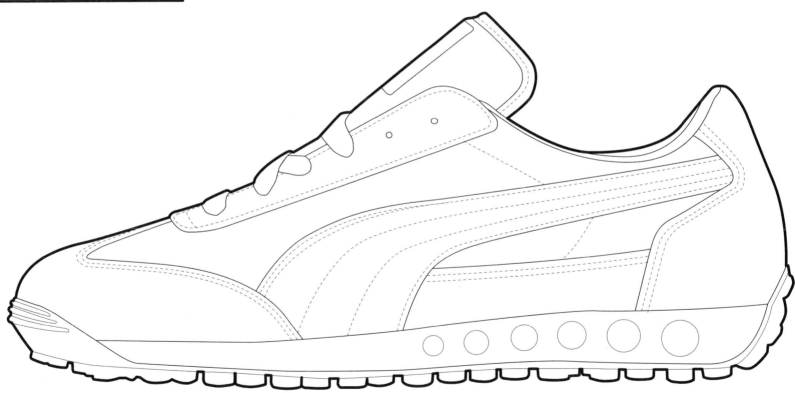

PUMA	
MODEL	EASY RIDER
LAUNCH	1982
CATEGORY	RUNNING
COLORIST	
DATE	

ADIDAS

MODEL	NEW YORK
LAUNCH	1983
CATEGORY	RUNNING

COLORIST	
DATE	

054

CONVERSE

MODEL	ALL STAR PRO STAR
LAUNCH	1983
CATEGORY	BASKETBALL
COLORIST	
DATE	

056

PUMA	
MODEL	CALIFORNIA
LAUNCH	1983
CATEGORY	TRAINING
COLORIST	
DATE	

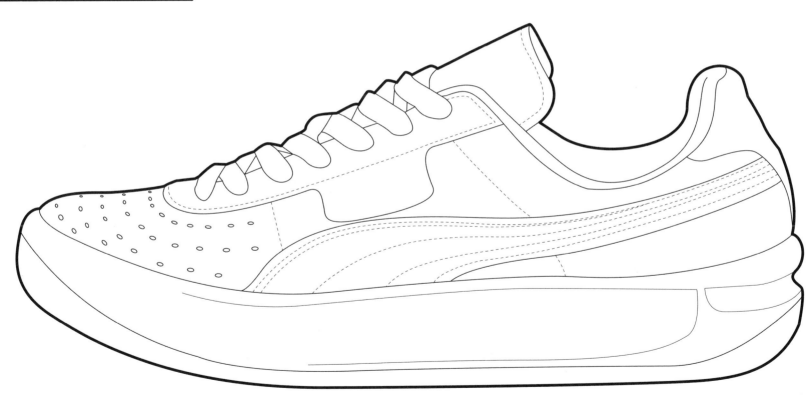

PUMA	
MODEL	FIRST ROUND
LAUNCH	1983
CATEGORY	BASKETBALL
COLORIST	
DATE	

058

PUMA	
MODEL	SKY II HI
LAUNCH	1983
CATEGORY	BASKETBALL
COLORIST	
DATE	

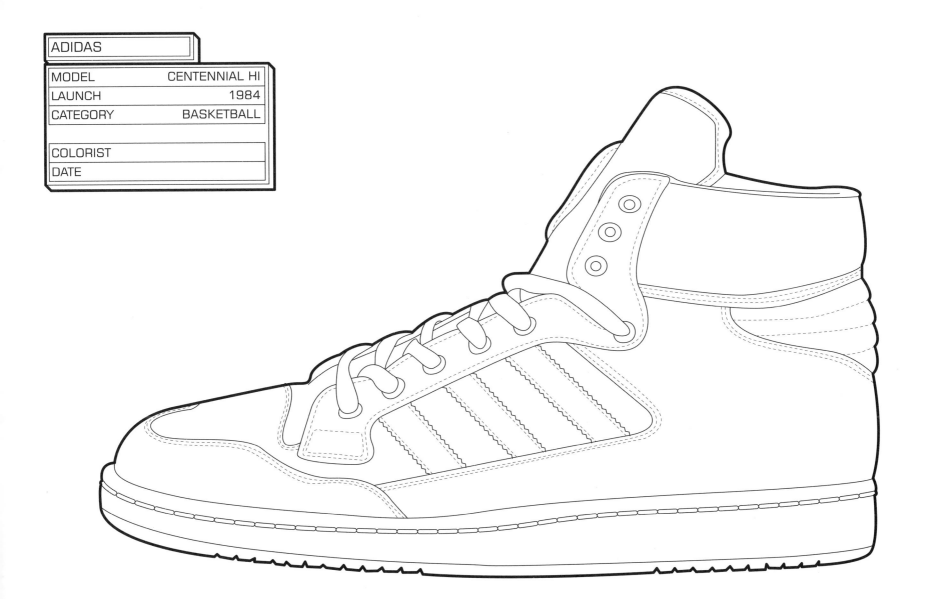

ADIDAS

MODEL	CENTENNIAL HI
LAUNCH	1984
CATEGORY	BASKETBALL

COLORIST	
DATE	

ADIDAS

MODEL	FORUM MID
LAUNCH	1984
CATEGORY	BASKETBALL

COLORIST	
DATE	

ADIDAS	
MODEL	LA TRAINER
LAUNCH	1984
CATEGORY	TRAINING
COLORIST	
DATE	

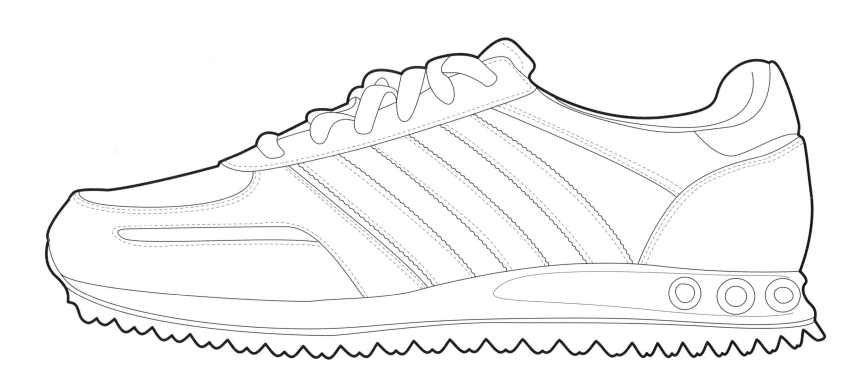

ADIDAS	
MODEL	RISING STAR
LAUNCH	1984
CATEGORY	TRAINING
COLORIST	
DATE	

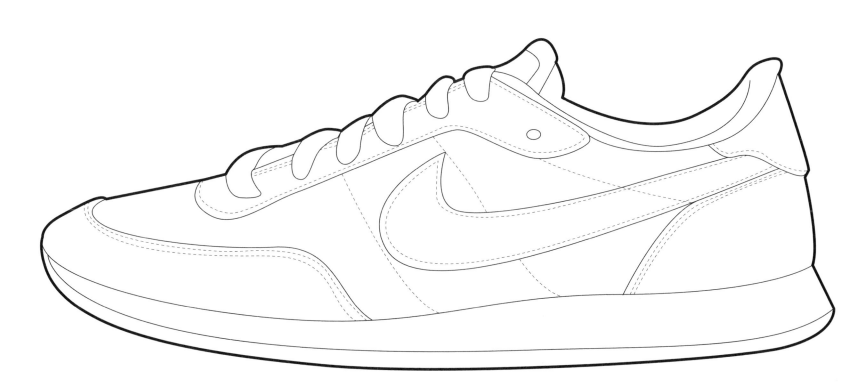

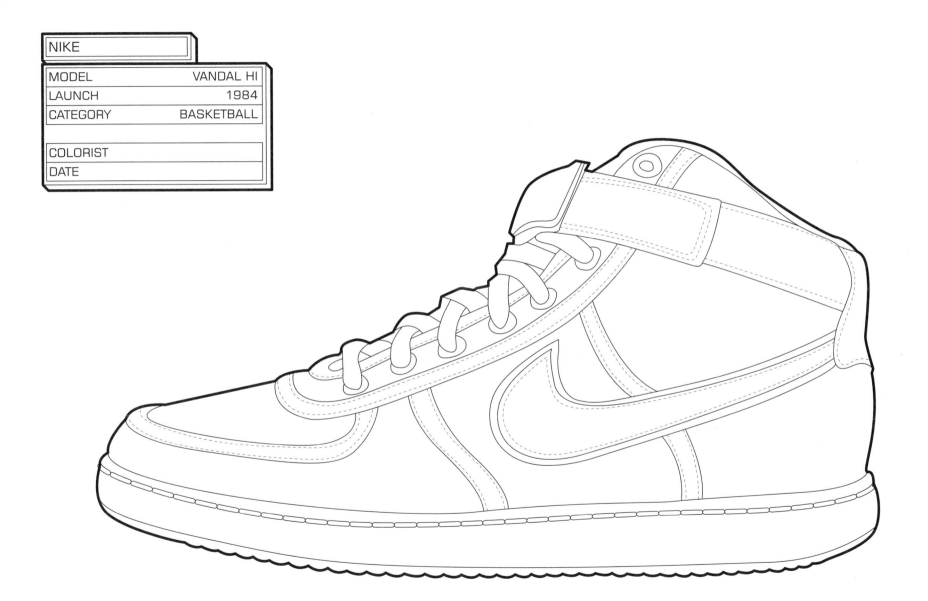

NIKE

MODEL	VANDAL HI
LAUNCH	1984
CATEGORY	BASKETBALL
COLORIST	
DATE	

PONY

MODEL	UPTOWN
LAUNCH	1984
CATEGORY	BASKETBALL

COLORIST	
DATE	

ADIDAS	
MODEL	ADICOLOR HI
LAUNCH	1985
CATEGORY	BASKETBALL
COLORIST	
DATE	

ADIDAS

MODEL	DECADE HI
LAUNCH	1985
CATEGORY	BASKETBALL

COLORIST	
DATE	

NIKE	
MODEL	AIR EPIC
LAUNCH	1985
CATEGORY	RUNNING
COLORIST	
DATE	

NIKE

MODEL	AIR JORDAN I
LAUNCH	1985
CATEGORY	BASKETBALL

COLORIST	
DATE	

NIKE	
MODEL	DUNK
LAUNCH	1985
CATEGORY	BASKETBALL
COLORIST	
DATE	

MODEL	FREESTYLE HI
LAUNCH	1985
CATEGORY	FITNESS

COLORIST	
DATE	

ADIDAS	
MODEL	ZX 500
LAUNCH	1986
CATEGORY	RUNNING
COLORIST	
DATE	

CONVERSE

MODEL	WEAPON
LAUNCH	1986
CATEGORY	BASKETBALL

COLORIST	
DATE	

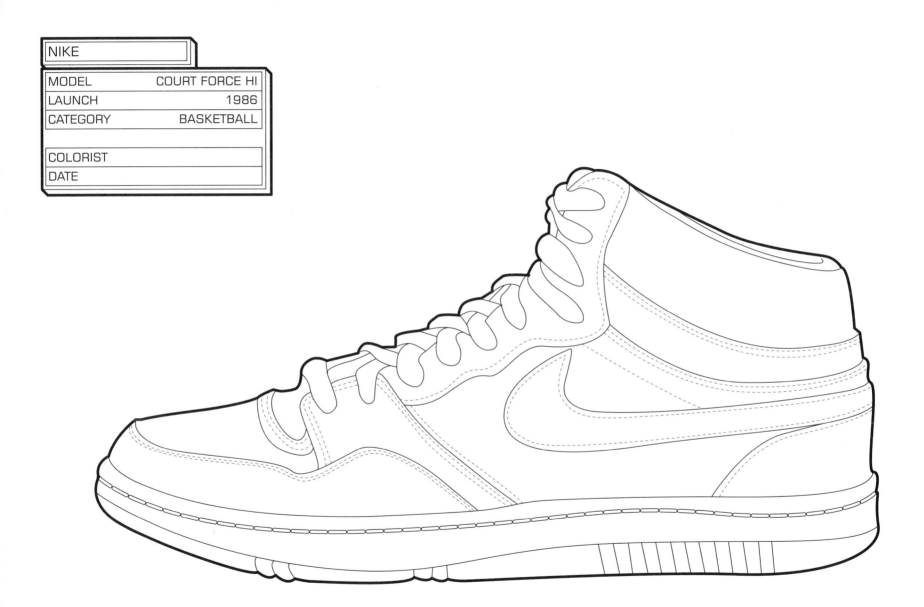

NIKE

MODEL	COURT FORCE HI
LAUNCH	1986
CATEGORY	BASKETBALL

COLORIST	
DATE	

ADIDAS	
MODEL	ZX 800
LAUNCH	1987
CATEGORY	RUNNING
COLORIST	
DATE	

NEW BALANCE

MODEL	M670
LAUNCH	1987
CATEGORY	RUNNING

COLORIST	
DATE	

NIKE	
MODEL	AIR MAX I
LAUNCH	1987
CATEGORY	RUNNING
COLORIST	
DATE	

NIKE	

MODEL	AIR SAFARI
LAUNCH	1987
CATEGORY	RUNNING

COLORIST	
DATE	

REEBOK	

MODEL	CLASSIC LEATHER
LAUNCH	1987
CATEGORY	RUNNING
COLORIST	
DATE	

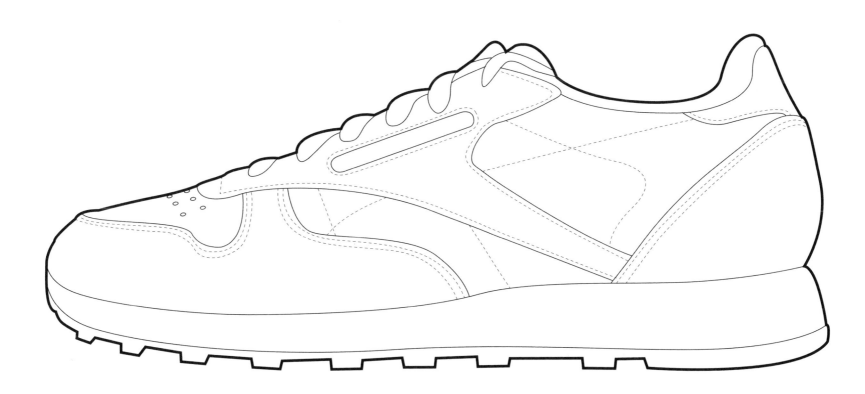

ADIDAS	
MODEL	ZX 8000
LAUNCH	1988
CATEGORY	RUNNING
COLORIST	
DATE	

FILA	
MODEL	FITNESS
LAUNCH	1988
CATEGORY	FITNESS
COLORIST	
DATE	

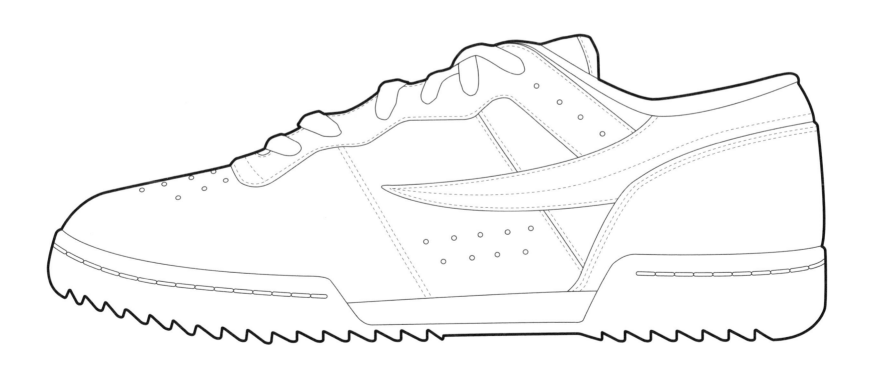

NIKE

MODEL	AIR REVOLUTION HI
LAUNCH	1988
CATEGORY	BASKETBALL
COLORIST	
DATE	

NIKE

MODEL	MULTI TRAINER
LAUNCH	1988
CATEGORY	TRAINING

| COLORIST | |
| DATE | |

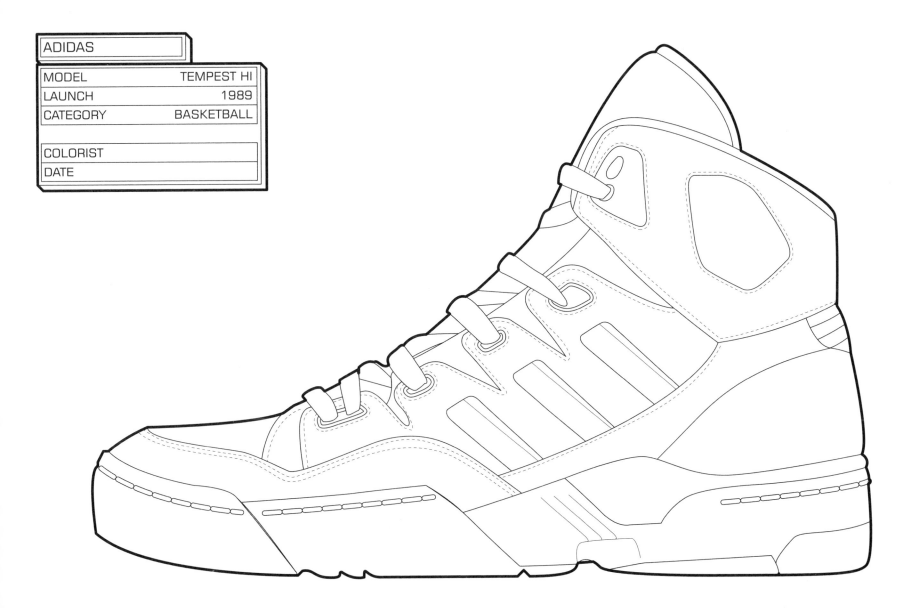

ADIDAS

MODEL	TEMPEST HI
LAUNCH	1989
CATEGORY	BASKETBALL

COLORIST	
DATE	

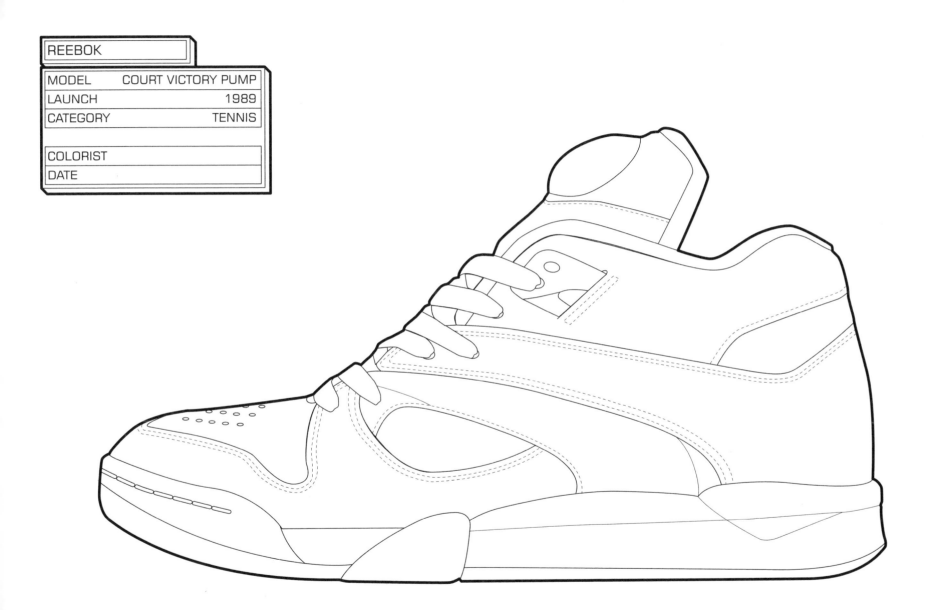

REEBOK

MODEL	COURT VICTORY PUMP
LAUNCH	1989
CATEGORY	TENNIS
COLORIST	
DATE	

NIKE	

MODEL	AIR CRAFT
LAUNCH	1990
CATEGORY	RUNNING

COLORIST	
DATE	

REEBOK

MODEL	COURT VICTORY DUAL
LAUNCH	1990
CATEGORY	TENNIS

COLORIST	
DATE	

REEBOK

MODEL	ERS 5000
LAUNCH	1990
CATEGORY	RUNNING

COLORIST	
DATE	

NEW BALANCE

MODEL	M997
LAUNCH	1991
CATEGORY	RUNNING

COLORIST	
DATE	

NIKE	
MODEL	AIR 180
LAUNCH	1991
CATEGORY	RUNNING
COLORIST	
DATE	

NIKE	
MODEL	AIR HUARACHE
LAUNCH	1991
CATEGORY	RUNNING
COLORIST	
DATE	

NIKE	
MODEL	AIR HUARACHE LIGHT
LAUNCH	1992
CATEGORY	RUNNING
COLORIST	
DATE	

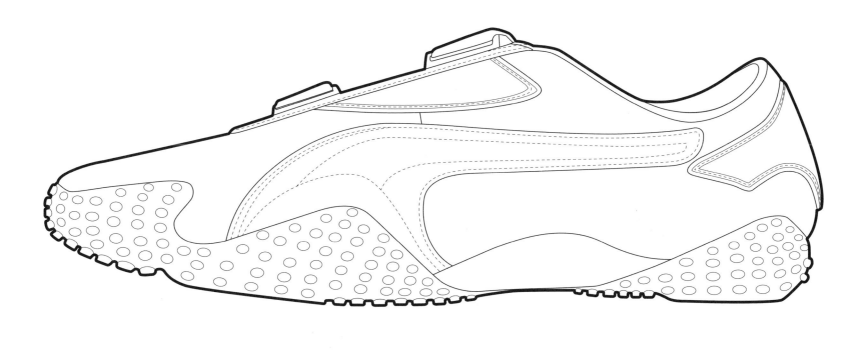

NIKE	
MODEL	AIR TRAINER ESCAPE
LAUNCH	2001
CATEGORY	RUNNING
COLORIST	
DATE	

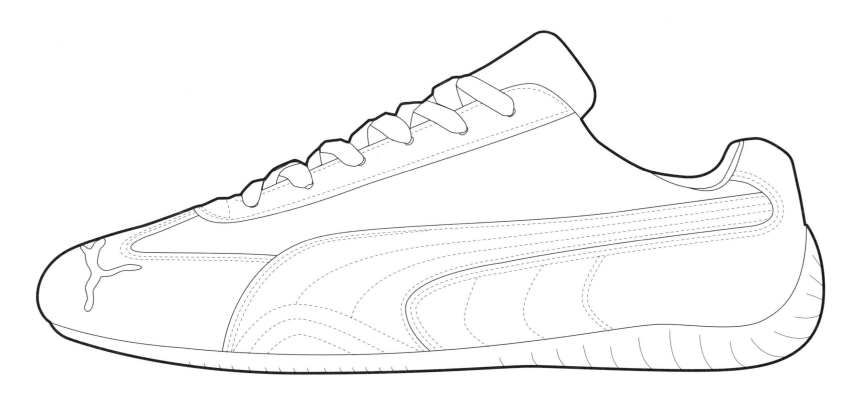

PUMA	
MODEL	SPEED CAT
LAUNCH	2001
CATEGORY	DRIVING
COLORIST	
DATE	

LE COQ SPORTIF	
MODEL	ESCRIME
LAUNCH	2002
CATEGORY	INDOOR
COLORIST	
DATE	

1900–1969

1970–1979

1980–1989

1990–TODAY

INDEX

Model:	Launch:	No.:		Model:	Launch:	No.:
Nike Air Max I	1987	079		Pro-Keds Court King	1955	004
Nike Air Pegasus	1989	088		Pro-Keds Shotmaker	1979	041
Nike Air Revolution Hi	1988	084				
Nike Air Safari	1987	080		Puma Argentina	1978	037
Nike Air Stab II	1988	085		Puma Cabana Racer	1981	048
Nike Air Trainer Escape	2001	098		Puma California	1983	057
Nike Blazer	1972	021		Puma Clyde	1968	016
Nike Challenge Court	1984	064		Puma Easy Rider	1982	052
Nike Cortez	1972	022		Puma First Round	1983	058
Nike Court Force Hi	1986	076		Puma Mostro	1999	097
Nike Dunk	1985	072		Puma Munich	1972	023
Nike Dynasty	1981	045		Puma RS 100	1972	024
Nike Multi Trainer	1988	086		Puma Sky II Hi	1983	059
Nike Oregon	1977	034		Puma Speed Cat	2001	099
Nike Rio	1984	065				
Nike Vandal Hi	1984	066		Reebok Classic Leather	1987	081
Nike Waffle Trainer	1973	025		Reebok Court Victory Dual	1990	091
				Reebok Court Victory Pump	1989	089
Onitsuka Tiger Fabre BL-L	1974	029		Reebok ERS 5000	1990	092
Onitsuka Tiger Mexico 66	1966	013		Reebok Freestyle Hi	1985	073
Onitsuka Tiger Nippon 60	1960	006				
Onitsuka Tiger Pro Gold 83	1983	056		Tretorn Nylite	1967	014
Onitsuka Tiger Runspark	1974	030				
Onitsuka Tiger Tai-Chi	1968	015		Vans Era	1976	033
Onitsuka Tiger Touch	1981	046		Vans SK8 Hi	1978	038
Onitsuka Tiger Ultimate 81	1981	047		Vans Slip-On	1973	026
Pony Three Ring Hi	1982	051				
Pony Top Star	1975	031				
Pony Uptown	1984	067				

We would like to point out that with a limit of 100 line arts we could not include the favorite model of all sport shoe enthusiasts. However, we are sure that we have included at least something for everyone.

We would like to thank everybody who helped make this book possible. Special thanks go to Laurence King Publishing, especially Jo Lightfoot, and Sophie Page for making it possible to publish a coloring book for big and small sneaker fans. We would also like to thank each department of the brands for their co-operation.

www.adidas.com
www.converse.com
www.dunlopfootwear.com.au
www.fila.com
www.kswiss.com
www.kawasakisko.dk
www.keds.com
www.lacoste.com
www.lecoqsportif.com
www.newbalance.com
www.nike.com
www.onitsukatiger.com
www.pony.com
www.prokeds.com
www.puma.com
www.reebok.com
www.tretorn.com
www.vans.com